DU[illegible]E

THE BIG DAY OUT BADGE

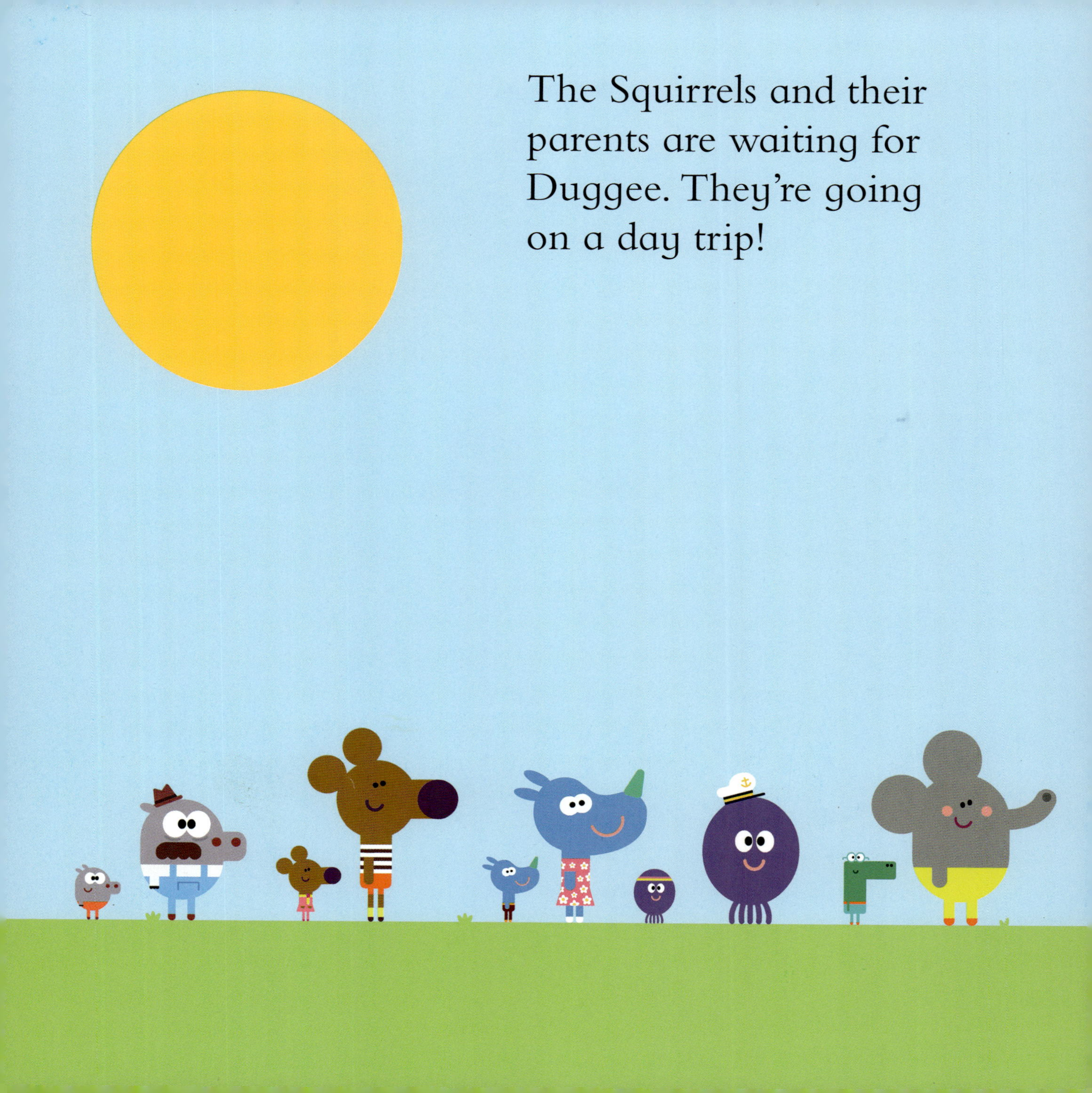

The Squirrels and their parents are waiting for Duggee. They're going on a day trip!

Here's Duggee! He's driving a bus. What fun!

"So, Duggee," says Norrie's dad. "I assume you have all the safety forms for this trip?"

Of course Duggee has all the safety forms. He's got his **Big Day Out Badge!**

Everyone buckles up.
The bus sets off.
"Where are we going?"
asks Betty.
"WOOF!" says Duggee.
It's a surprise!

The bus is driving past the famous Rainbow Rocks.

Duggee shakes his head. They are going somewhere much better!

The Squirrels see some wombats waving outside a wobbly watermill.

"Are we going here, Duggee?" asks Tag. No! The bus drives on.

The Squirrels see King Gallivant looking down from his castle.

"Are we going here, Duggee?" asks Betty. No! The bus drives on.

The bus drives past all sorts of amazing places. Duggee drives on to Bagpipe Bridge. It's not too far now!

The Squirrels wave to
a friendly monster.

Suddenly, the bridge huffs and puffs . . .
just like bagpipes!
The bus bounces off the bridge and
back on to the open road.

At last, Duggee stops driving. He parks the bus in an empty green field.

Norrie's dad scratches his head. "But, Duggee," he says, frowning, "you said that we were going somewhere special?"

This IS somewhere special. It is Duggee's special picnic spot! Everybody takes a seat.

Duggee turns on his radio. He hands out jam sandwiches and blueberry juice. Duggee makes the BEST jam sandwiches!

Duggee's picnic spot is perfect.
Betty and her dad even spot some
blue-billed beatboxing birds.

The blue-billed beatboxing birds start to boogie to Duggee's music.

Sir Gallivant arrives, and so does the monster from Bagpipe Bridge. They want to join the picnic too!

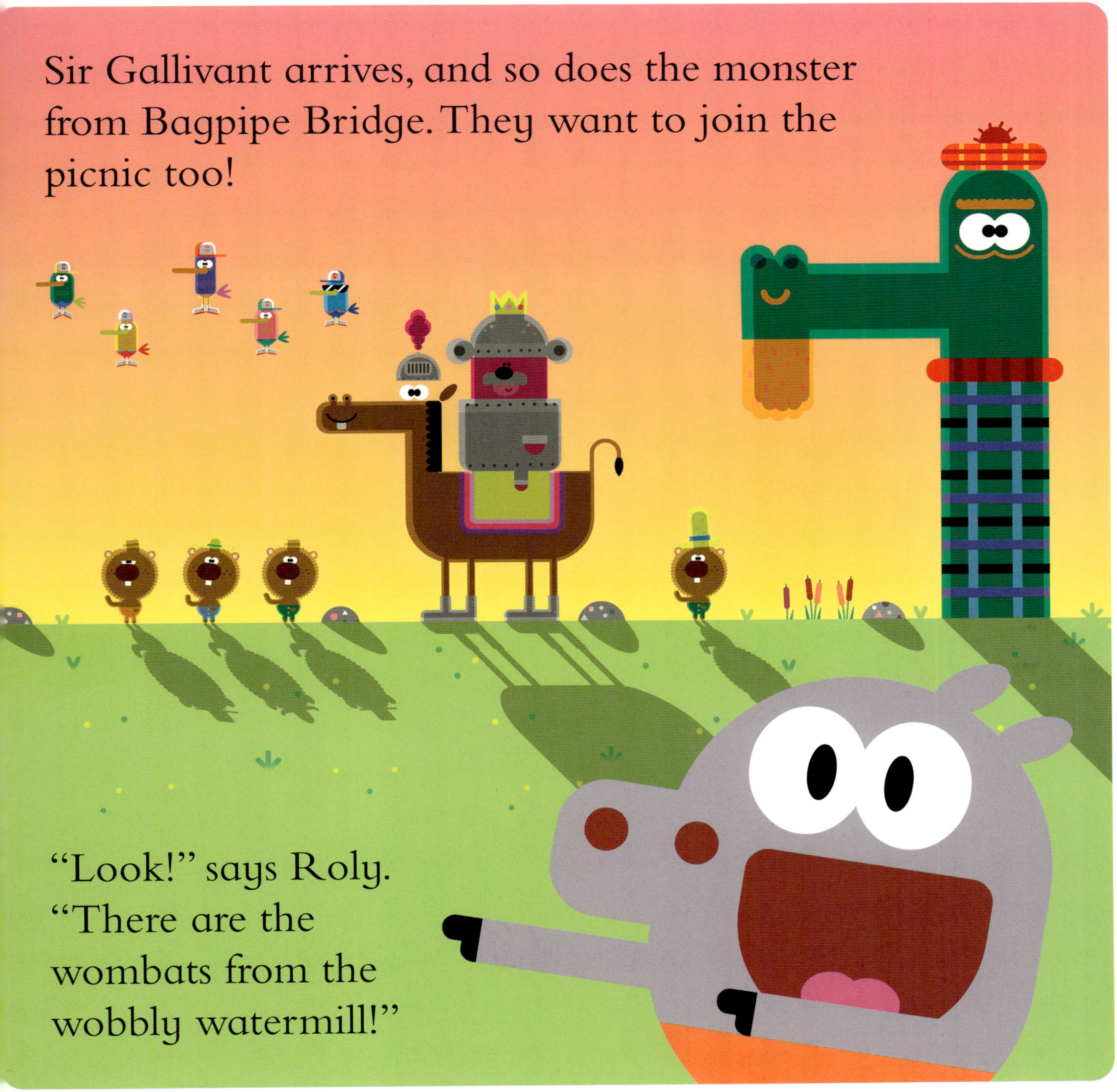

"Look!" says Roly. "There are the wombats from the wobbly watermill!"

Soon, EVERYONE is dancing to Duggee's disco beat!

The music gets louder and louder until . . . *CLICK!* Duggee switches off the radio.

Everybody stops dancing.

It’s time to go home now, everyone!
“Awww!” cry the Squirrels and their parents.

Well done, Squirrels. You've earned your **Big Day Out Badges!**

Now there's just time for one last thing before the Squirrels go home . . .

"DUGGEE HUG!"